Contents

Contents

CYBER CRIMES, LAW, AND CYBER-FORENSICS: COMPARATIVE STUDY OF INDIA, UK, AND USA

VOLUME 2, ISSUE 3 OF BRILLOPEDIA

MANISH KUMAR AND APOORVA THAKUR

Made with ♥ on the Notion Press Platform
www.notionpress.com

Preface

"Start writing, no matter what. The water does not flow until the faucet is turned on".

- Louis L'Amour

Hundreds of students and professors are contributing their work to Brillopedia, we are here to provide ample information about Law and Contemporary issues. Our aim is to provide a platform for today's generation to express their views and ideas on law and contemporary law.

Authors

Advocate Manish Kumar (LL.M) has 15+ years of criminal litigation experience (as in 2022) in the Courts of Delhi-NCR, and corporate advisory across India and abroad.
Apart from being an actively practising defence counsel, he is even a certified PoCSO-Trainer, and also takes keen interest in the domains of Block-Chain and Artificial Intelligence (AI), Energy Laws, Data-Protection, Labour Law-Compliances, and White-collar crimes.
Advocate Kumar is the Founder-Managing Partner of the New Delhi-based law firm, MKA Legal Law Offices, and also serves as Co-Director at the registered non-profit company, LAWGYSTIX Foundation.
He may be contacted at +91-9910479847 or manish.mkalegal@gmail.com

Advocate Apoorva Thakur (LL.M, NET) has 9+ years of PQE in the legal field (as in 2022), primarily consisting of lawyering and teaching experience in Delhi-NCR, with IP advisory across India and overseas.
A certified PoSH Enabler, she is also a qualified Assistant Professor, NABET and SQA-backed TTT-certified Soft-Skill Trainer, Image Consultant, Etiquette Coach, and Mentor to bootstrapped start-ups and women and child-related NGOs.
She takes keen interest in Gender Sensitization Advocacy, Wildlife Protection and Environment Conservation Regulations, and in the interplay between IPR and Entertainment Laws.
A Partner at MKA Legal Law Offices, Ms. Thakur heads LAWGYSTIX Foundation as its Director.
She may be contacted at +91-9599023102 or advapoorvathakur@gmail.com

Publication

This research paper is published in volume 2, issue 3 of Brillopedia

CHAPTER ONE

ABSTRACT

New forms of crime have emerged with the rising prevalence of computer misuse. Some of them employ cutting-edge tools and methods for criminal conspiracy. From spreading fraud through email to stealing and illegally reselling intellectual property, cybercrime covers a lot of ground in the present-day world. The domain of computer-science known as "cyber forensics" is considered to be one of the most essential subfields of cyber law in present times. It is concerned with the investigation of cybercrimes. Its objective is mainly to conduct an examination of electronic content in a manner that is forensically sound with the goals of preserving, recovering, analyzing, identifying, and presenting facts and views about digital information.

This paper focuses on the significance of the topic chosen alongside emphasis upon the methods and instruments that are used by cyber forensic investigators. Cyber forensics evidence undergoes the same processes as other digital evidence, and serves as supporting evidence in judicial proceedings. This research-work demonstrates the necessity for further investigation into how cyber forensics might be used to enhance the identification of cybercrimes. The authors intend to fill some gaps in our knowledge of how laws utilize cyber forensic investigations in India, United Kingdom, and United States of Americato unearth and address cybercrimes. In the process, this work, involving doctrinal study,also aims to explore cyber-security policiesexisting in the three aforementioned jurisdictions to identify similarities and differences in all three – thus broadening the base of research and paving a path for future study on the same theme.

Keywords: Cybercrime, Cyber Forensics, Digital, Policy, Cyber-security

CHAPTER TWO

INTRODUCTION

The increasing need for massive data-storage is driven by the exponential expansion of the internet.Technology has given rise to a new genre of criminal activity: cybercrimes.With the proliferation of personal computing devices like smartphones, the number of cybercrime casesis on an all-time rise. Hacking, bank-fraud, and email-spamming are just some of the many crimes that may be examined by cyber-forensic investigators.

Cybercrime includes any illegal activity that involves the use of the internet or any other electronic means to disrupt the normal operation of a computer or computer network. The computer may or may not have played a significant role in the conduct of the crime, but both the computer and the network are considered to fall under the radar of investigators. It broadly refers to any kind of criminal activity involving the electronic processing and transfer of data that occurs inside a computer-system.[1]

Since computers and also the internet is used in almost every aspect of modern life (banks, communications, travel, infrastructure, healthcare, entertainment, legal sector, etc.), this type of crime has exploded in recent years. The problems associated with this sort of crime, such as hacking, intellectual property theft, data-leaks, pornography, morphing, etc., have recently risen to the forefront. When private information is unlawfully or accidentally captured, published, or leaked, it creates privacy issues – another huge concern in today's times.[2]

The potential to participate in espionage, money-theft, and various cross-border crimes, commonly referred to as 'cyber warfare', is growing in relevance for both State and non-State actors on a worldwide scale. The International Criminal Court is one of the few institutions aiming to address this issue by bringing those responsible to justice.

Many modern electronic gadgets, including storage devices, video-game consoles, etc. can receive data from the user, transmit it somewhere, and also store it. This information or the use of such tools forms the crude foundation of cyber-forensics. Collating, analysing, and reporting digital evidence in a way that complies with the law falls within this branch of knowledge. It may be useful in cases involving forensic evidence, such as those encompassing the identification or prevention of criminal activity. However, cyber-forensic investigation extends beyond the data collecting and storage methods typically used by end-users and IT support-personnel. Like traditional forensics, cyber-forensics is essentially the study of how the law may be applied to computer technology. Preserving, identifying, extracting, and documenting evidence from cyberspace defines its primary domain of functioning. The precision of evidence-retention and the accuracy of data-processing outcomes is paramount in cyber-forensics, much like in other forensic disciplines.

[1] Dr. R. K. Chaubey, "An Introduction to Cyber Crime & Cyber Law" (Kamal Law House Kolkata)(2008).

[2] Vakul Sharma, "Handbook of Cyber Law" (Macmillan)(2002).

CHAPTER THREE

BACKGROUND OF CYBER-FORENSICS AND RELATION TO LAW

"Crime by Computer," written by Donn Parker in 1976, is widely regarded as the first depiction of the use of electronic information in the investigation and prosecution of computer-aided crimes. Back then, most systems were not heavily networked to the outside world; therefore, it was the responsibility of system-administrators to ensure the safety of their systems. Audits of the system were developed to check the precision of data-processing - a costly endeavour in those times. This auditing process amounted to the first-ever comprehensive attempt at ensuring computer safety. The outcome of these efforts was the ability to utilize audit-data in investigations of possible malfeasance. *Ad hoc* organisations of volunteer law-enforcement officers were formed by agencies, including the Department of Defense (DoD), the Internal Revenue Service (IRS), and the Federal Bureau of Investigation (FBI); and these were imparted basic training on mainframe and mini-computers. These cyber-forensic experts would aid other case-investigators in retrieving information and accessing records from mainframe systems. In most cases, detectives with computer-expertise would team up with network-administrators.[1]

In the case of a suspected breach of security, Government employees were tasked with guarding sensitive information, and they teamed with cyber-forensic experts not only to gain help towards forensic investigations and determine the nature of breach, but also to gain insights into how such breaches may be avoided in the future. Eventually, cyber-forensics, which investigates and responds to high-tech crimes, and the information security sector, which safeguards data and assets, merged into a single discipline. Over the decades that followed, and up to the present, the discipline still continues to develop. Both public and commercial institutions have either begun employing dedicated and in-house cyber-forensic and information security experts, or outsourcing their tasks to external specialists. The necessity for cyber forensics studies in civil law disputes was recently recognised by the private law domain – thus leading to a boom in the area of rediscovering criminal laws.[2]

As a field, cyber forensics can be traced back to 1984, with the creation of the FBI's "Magnetic Media programme", which would eventually become known as the "Computer Analysis and Response Team (CART)". The International Association of Computer Investigative Specialists (IACIS) was founded in 1988 as a non-profit organisation, with the mission of educating and certifying cyber-forensic experts worldwide. After this, in 1995, the International Organization for Computer Evidence (IOCE) was formed to facilitate communication and collaboration among groups working with electronic evidence, and to guarantee uniformity and quality in the forensics industry. With the rise of cyber-attacks, the G-8 nations decided, in 1997, that "law-enforcement officers must be taught and equipped to cope with it",thus emphasising the necessity of cyber-forensics. In 1998, the G-8 gave IICE, the task of developing standards for digital evidence around the globe. In the same year, INTERPOL had its Forensic Science Symposium. In the year 2000, the FBI opened its first regional cyber-forensics laboratory in San Diego.[3]

[1] Dr. Vishwanath Paranjape, "Legal Dimensions of Cybercrimes and Preventive Laws", Central Law Agency (2010).

[2] Dr. Amita Verma, "Cyber Crimes and Law" (Central Law Publications)(2009).

[3]*Ibid*

CHAPTER FOUR

USE OF CYBER-FORENSICS IN LAW: WHY, WHEN, HOW

Evidence on a computer may be collected and preserved with the help of cyber-forensics. This branch of knowledge is often used to unearth material that may be presented as proof in a legal proceeding. There are many fields outside law-enforcement that fall under the umbrella of cyber-security. Professionals in this industry may sometimes be asked to rescue inaccessible files from dead hard-drives, broken servers, or wiped operating-systems.

Once a cybercrime is reported, one of the first places where an investigator seeks evidence is the suspect's electronic devices, such as his/her/its computer or mobile-phone. A specialist in cyber-forensics might be helpful in this situation. The device is usually seized as evidence and examined by the expert. Stringent protocols are adhered to while investigations are underway, to provide admissible evidence. Whatever they find—papers, history of sites visited, or even metadata—could be utilised as evidence in a case against the accused.

Professionals in the domain of cyber-forensics are not limited to only gathering of evidence; they may also engage in data-recovery, as mentioned above. Apart from helping find criminal evidence, this is even helpful for anybody who has lost critical information, such as firms that may have suffered a system-meltdown, etc.[1]

The goal of cyber-forensics is to piece together what occurred, who was involved, and when it happened - by examining data generated by or stored in computer-systems. This procedure locates, retrieves, examines, and stores electronically-retained material for future retrieval and potential use as evidence in court-proceedings.

Examples of common situations in which cyber-forensics is used, include the follows:

- Data-breach;
- Theft of intellectual property;
- White-collar offences;
- Online frauds;
- Cyber-stalking or bullying;
- Child-pornography;
- Morphing;
- MMS-leaks;
- Cyber-defamations[2]

[1]Niya John, "Developments in Information Technology", Medium (March 6, 2018) <https://medium.com/@niyajohn9495/developments-in-information-technology-b93c74b7bd79>, accessed on October 26, 2022.

[2] "When Would Computer Forensics Be Used? | Computer Forensics NZ" (*Computer Forensics NZ*, September 11, 2021) <http://www.datarecovery.co.nz/forensic-investigation/when-would-computer-forensics-be-used> accessed on October 26, 2022.

CHAPTER FIVE

CYBER-FORENSICINVESTIGATIONS AND DIGITAL EVIDENCE

Forensics is the art and science of discovering ideas, extracting and conserving them, and presenting them in a court of law. The elementary steps in cyber-forensics include- to evaluate the occurrence, analyze the method of operation behind the crime, and make a list of all conceivable locations where the evidence could be found. Computer-forensics, mobile-forensics, network-forensicsall form part of cyber-forensics. Digital-forensics is divided into four stages- Collection, Examination, Analysis, Reporting.

Forensic analysis of data-storage devices must be performed using software-tools for undeleting deleted files, breaking passwords of secured files, decrypting encrypted information, and so on.One leading tool used, is 'Encase'. "

Cyber-Forensics includes:

- Outlining the source of the email;
- Finding and decrypting password-protected information;
- Recovering deleted data;
- Careful identification and classification of all items including cables, peripherals, and external storage-media;
- Noting the time shown on the computer's built-in clock;
- Videographing the computers where they are now located, paying close attention to the wiring of any add-ons and extras;
- Appropriate events for safe shutting-down of machines that are operating at the time of the attack"

Here, it becomes relevant to discuss also about ‘eDiscovery’. This refers to the process of exploring potential solutions for a company. Legal standards for the administration and admissibility of electronic discovery evidence must be satisfied, and the process must be repeatable and standardised. For instance, e-Discovery may benefit from the addition of ‘email archiving’. It is a discovery process that can be relied upon in court-proceedings, can be repeated with accuracy, provides sufficient relevant information, and complies with all applicable laws and regulations regarding the handling and admissibility of digital evidence. Finding, collecting, preserving, processing, examining, and producing relevant material stored electronically are all part of a successful e-discovery process.[1]

When a hard-disc has to be analyzed for suggestions, there could be inadvertent data-corruption or an allegation of data-manipulation. As a result, the investigator does no forensic analysis of the original hard-disc that he has confiscated. The investigator typically builds a clone of the detained hard-disc, which is a bit of an Image Copy of the suspicious disc, and then analyses it. The duplication is carried out in the presence of witnesses, preferably the disk’s owner. For each questionable disc, at least two cloned discs are generated; one is returned to the disc-user, while the original is sealed for submission to the Court. It should be noted that even deleted data can be read by scientific software capable of reading binary data at the byte level. Even when a disc is reformatted using high-level formatting, the data is not destroyed, and is thus retrievable.[2]

The data that is used by a computer while it is turned on and then discarded when the machine is turned off, is termed as ‘volatile data’, which is normally stored in RAM (Random Access Memory) space. Needless to say, before shutting down the computer, an investigator should try to understand what is insidethe concerned computer’s volatile memory by using tools that swiftly analyze the RAM. Analyzing the RAM may shed important insightsinto previous and current network associates, which is crucial when determining the remote destination/s with which the malware is/might have been connecting, the source of child pornography, and so on. ‘Mem Marshal 1.0’ is a popular forensic-application that supports RAM-examination in Windows XP computers.[3]

Investigating and analysing databases and their information is the subject of ‘database forensics’, a branch of cyber-forensics. Forensic database-analysis may make use of row-level timestamps (update timings) in a relational table to verify the authenticity of user operations.[4]

Mobile-Forensics comprises data-extraction from SIM cards or data cards, as well as data-extraction from mobile hardware, including erased data. A gadget like this is called 'Cellebrite.' SMS and MMS are important types of information obtained through mobile phones. Service-benefactor logs and call-data records are vital additional shreds of evidence that can be gathered. With the fast-paced field of GPS Forensics, Mobile Device Forensics, also known as "SatNav Forensics", is a relatively young discipline. It is used to examine and analyse GPS devices to recover data such as Routes, Photos, Audio, TrackPoints, TrackLogs, WayPoints, and so on.[5]

To add to this, as regards 'IP Tracing', there is a plethora of softwares available which resolve IP addresses and also display the typical flow of data via the internet. 'Trace Route' is a popular example of such a tool.

Network-Forensics, another significant form of cyber-forensics,entails encountering digital evidence distributed across computer-networks. Wireless-forensics is a subset of the larger discipline of network-forensics. It aims to provide investigators with the resources they need to capture and analyse data from wireless network-traffic. The information gathered may be basic statistics, or indicative of the broad use of Voice over Internet Protocol (VoIP) systems, especially those that employ wireless-networking. One must be wary of the risks involved in gathering evidence through a network. Because of how rapidly logs may evolve, crucial data might vanish within seconds of beginning a log-study. Getting evidence from some sources, such as Internet Service Providers (ISPs), may need permission.

This process can take time, which increases the chances of evidence-loss. Other pitfalls include the following:[6]

- A normal computer or network activity may seem like an attack to an investigator or system administrator;
- The continuity of signs may be broken at certain points;
- There is a chance that logs are unspecific, missing, or incomplete;
- Other countries may be engaged in the probe due to the global nature of the Internet That might cause problems for the probe on the legal and political fronts."

Malware-Forensics, yet another form of cyber-forensics, is concerned with the analysis and detection of malicious codes - to study their payload, viruses, worms, Trojans, key-loggers, and so on.

E-mails, calendars, and contacts (even those that have been deleted) may often be recovered and analysed by way of 'Email Forensics'."A typical forensic-lab for such purpose consists of three important divisions:

- Data-Acquisition Division- Is rresponsible for picking up sanitized hard-disks for data-acquisition and cloning the suspect hard-disk into sanitized hard-disks;
- Data-Analysis Division- Analyses the data and makes reports;
- Data-Custody Division- Is Responsible for storing the disk in a protected safe (free from external magnetic influences) and for transmission of disks in properly packaged condition to avoid corruption in transit.

[1] B.B. Nanda & Dr. R.K. Tewari, "Cyber Crime - A Challenge to Forensic Science", The Indian Journal, pg. 102 to 103 (April-September, 2000).

[2]A.S. Chawla, "Cyber Crime Investigation & Prevention", The Police Journal (April-September, 2016).

[3]Dr. Swarupa Dholam, "Cyber Law in Developing Countries: An Indian Perspective",Journal of the Colloquium for Information System Security Education (September 2016) <file:///C:/Users/Admin/Downloads/ curator,+CISSE_v04_i01_p02%20(1).pdf >, accessed on October 29, 2022.

[4]*Ibid*

[5]*Ibid*

[6]*Ibid*

CHAPTER SIX

COMPARATIVE STUDY OF CYBER LAWS AND CYBER-FORENSICS – INDIA, UK, AND USA

India

According to CERT-IN, in every ten minutes, a new cybercrime was recorded in India last year. Authorities should work together to counteract this worrying trend.

Once confined to computer hacking alone, cybercrime has recently expanded to encompass data-theft, ransomware, child pornography, and many other forms of online wrongdoing. Crypto-jacking (the practice of secretly installing malware on a victim's computer for mining cryptocurrency without the user's knowledge) is also growing steadily.

Some other dangers that may occur on the web include information-disclosure, industrial sabotage, and the loss of privacy through IT transfers.[1]

In India, it is also common nowadays to mislead someone about the origin of a communication by sending it over a single telecommunications network, delivering an improper message, or using a digital document - all examples of a type of cyber-cheating. Also, trying to steal email-signatures or identities (including the use of another netizen's passcodes or authentication system), or hijacking computer-systems or other telecommunication technologies – fall under serious cybercrimes. Criminal violations of Section 66, IT Act of 2000 are cognizable, and the accused is not even entitled to the right of bail.[2] With the passage of the Computer

Crime Act in 2005, India's basic law regarding information technology was brought up-to-date.

Under the definition of "technology" in the Indian Penal Code (IPC), digital recordings and papers are treated the same way as physical documentations. Sections 464, 469, 467, 471, 475, 477, 478 IPC which deal with the fraudulent entry in a register, or wrong paperwork, have been amended to include the words "digital record and excel spreadsheet," bringing them in sync with the IT legislation. To commit acts of forgery or fabrication of record-keeping is a crime in India, and it is now legal to use digital records and computer-files instead of traditional paperwork.

To ensure that the necessary paper-records can be protected and proven under either the IPC or the IT Amendment Act, investigating organisations must diligently file cases and chargesheets citing the relevant portions of both the laws. In cases involving similar offences, this includes Sections 464, 467, 469 and 470 of the IPC, as well as Sections 43 and 69 of the IT Amendment Act.

It was only possible to present physical evidence in Court before the IT Act was passed in 2000. This formalised the validity of digital documents and electronic evidences in India. Section 68B of the Act, which codified the acceptance of electronic document-authentication as evidence, was a ground-breaking reform. The term "papers" under the definitions in the Indian Evidence Act has been expanded to encompass "any papers constituting digital records".

"Digital certificate", "digital form", "secure digital document", and "digital signature" are all examples of terminology that were introduced to create the backbone of the legislation's evidentiary relevance in today's times of technological revolution.[3]

United Kingdom

In the UK, there is a lack of unified legislation that holistically addressesthe concern of cybersecurity. The Computer Misuse Act (CMA), 1990 made it illegal to tamper with a computer without permission; the Investigatory Powers Act (IPA), 2016 made it illegal to intercept communications, including communications sent or received by computers; and the General Data Protection Regulation (GDPR), 2016 made it mandatory for organisations to take reasonable precautions to protect data of individuals and organizations domiciled in Europe. Other relevant legislations include the Data Protection Act (DPA), 2018; the Network and Information Systems Regulation (NISR), 2018"; the Fraud Act, 2006; and the Intellectual Property Rights Enforcement Act (IPREA), which makes it illegal to infringe on Copyrights, Designs and Patents registered in the UK; and the Proceeds of Crime Act (PoCA), 2002, to prevent criminals from benefitting from data-related offences.[4]

As regards cybersecurity, the primary focus of British law is on deterrence via punishment (most notably, to address the failure of data-controllers and processors to keep personal data safe).[5]

The DPA expands upon, supplements, and offers exemptions from the GDPR. With few exceptions, the DPA makes it a crime to deliberately or recklessly access or disclose personal data without the agreement of the Controller. It also controls how agencies like the Serious Fraud Office, Financial Conduct Authority, and National Crime Agency handle personal information.

It is a violation of the CMA for a person to cause a computer to perform any function with the intent to secure access to any programme or data held in any computer, or to enable any such access to be secured, if the access he or she intends to secure or enable is unauthorised, and the person knows at the time the function is caused that the access is unauthorised. Due to the extreme nature of the damage they inflict or the threat they represent to national security, several of these crimes may receive a sentence of life in prison.

There are a wide variety of methods for protecting data on a computer or inside the software. In the CMA, the word "computer" is not defined. Unauthorized access occurs when someone other than the person responsible for the computer and authorised to make such a determination gains access to the system.

The CMA adds new offences when unauthorised access is used to commit other crimes like theft or fraud or to damage the functionality of a computer (such as installing viruses or spyware). Ten years in prison is the maximum punishment for such an offence. It is also a crime under the CMA to purchase, manufacture, alter, provide, or sell anything that may be used to commit a crime under the CMA.

United States of America

No federal legislation in the USA addresses data security, privacy, or cyber-security as a whole. In addition to the federal regulations, some states in USA have passed their own cyber-security legislations. As a result, there is a patchwork of federal and state rules that may have widely different effects. American technology leadership and e-commerce have both contributed to a rise in cybercrimes. Significant growth in data-breaches happened as a consequence of digitalization of the financial sector, hospitals, and small and medium-sized businesses (SMEs).[6]Between 2005 and 2015, more than 500 million records in USA were exposed due to data-breaches. In 2016, USA witnessed 1093 data-breaches, leading to the unfortunate loss of 36 million pieces of vital records and information! To improve cyber defences, former US President,Mr. Obama,had signed the Cybersecurity Enhancement Act (CSA) on December 18, 2014. Efforts are being made by both Government and businesses to improve cyber-security training and study for the public in USA.

In California, the Personal Information Protection Act of 2003 endeavors to protect a company's reputation and financial losses if it invested in cyber-security measures.[7]

The consequences for criminals who get access to private data of New York's residents and businesses might be severe.

Other important federal cyber-security legislations include the Health Insurance Portability and Accountability Act (HIPAA), the Gramm-Leach-Bliley Act (GLBA), and the Homeland Security Act (HSA). In response to current cyber-dangers, federal authorities have developed many steps to assist businesses in properly securing their data. However, administration-networks are still vulnerable to hacking despite legislative and governmental attempts to prevent it. The same is also true for non-public enterprises. The safety of a company's most vital records and software is a top priority, especially in light of the fact that cyber-criminals ceaselessly launch increasingly sophisticated assaults everyday!

[1]"Cyber Laws of India - ISEA" (ISEA) <https://www.infosecawareness.in/cyber-laws-of-india>, accessed onOctober29, 2022

[2] Madhyama Subramanian, "India: Promoting Internet Safety amongst Netizens" <https://www.unodc.org/southasia/frontpage/2012/May/india_-addressing-the-rise-of-cybercrime-amongst-children.html>, accessed on October 29, 2022

[3]*Supra*, Note 1

[4] "Cybersecurity in United Kingdom (England & Wales) - Lexology" (*Lexology*) <https://www.lexology.com/library/detail.aspx?g=09262dc8-609b-45b1-bba9-8291f6d9c112>, accessed on October 27, 2022.

[5]*Ibid*

[6] EES, "Cybersecurity Laws and Regulations in US 2022 - EES Corporation" (*EES Corporation*, November 4, 2021) <https://www.eescorporation.com/cybersecurity-laws-and-regulations-in-us/>, accessed on October 28, 2022.

[7] "Homeland Security Act | United States [2002]" (*Encyclopedia Britannica*)https://www.britannica.com/topic/Homeland-Security-Act, accessed on October 28, 2022

CHAPTER SEVEN

CONCLUSION

Cybercrime poses real risks, and it is up to us as a society to make sure awareness is spread worldwide as regards online safety. Greater knowledge about cyber-security threats would be a good step forward. The battleground of the future will be the Internet. There has to be an international agreement on cybercrime-deterrence, and all nations need to take the necessary measures to make that happen.

Future years will certainly witness an increased reliance on computers. Because of this, we should expect a parallel rise in the crime-rate over cyberspace as well, since the number of people utilizing technology is bound to grow exponentially. Investigations about cybercrimes must be meticulous if the truth is to be uncovered in all such matters. It is crucial to provide training for law-enforcement agencies and judicial officers. Sharpening and innovating practises related to prosecuting instances of computer-based criminality is essential if we are to approach such offences/ wrongs with a 'military mindset'. For deterrence purposes, the system must allow for severe punishment for computer-crimes. Punishments and penalties need to be enhanced and made harsher. For efficient tracking and documentation of computer cases, a separate Bench composed of impartial members is required especially in all developing countries.

To conclude, since the growth and improvement of electronic systems is intrinsically linked to the long-term development of our society, we must endeavour to pay more attention to this alarming evil bound to become uglier with the passage of time and technological developments.

Printed by Libri Plureos GmbH in Hamburg,
Germany